Salty Dogs

Salty Dogs

JEAN M. FOGLE

Wiley Publishing, Inc.

Howell Book House
Published by Wiley Publishing, Inc., Hoboken, New Jersey

For general information on our other products and services or to obtain technical support please contact our Customer Care Department within the U.S. at (800) 762-2974, outside the U.S. at (317) 572-3993 or fax (317) 572-4002.

Wiley also publishes its books in a variety of electronic formats. Some content that appears in print may not be available in electronic books. For more information about Wiley products, please visit our web site at www.wiley.com.

Library of Congress Cataloging-in-Publication Data:
Fogle, Jean M., 1952–
Salty dogs / Jean M. Fogle.
       p.   cm.
       ISBN-13: 978-0-470-16904-9 (cloth)
       ISBN-10: 0-470-16904-4
       1. Dogs—Pictorial works.   2. Beaches—Pictorial works.   I. Title.
       SF430.F64   2007
       636.70022 ' 2—dc22

                                     2007015330

Printed in China

10 9 8 7 6 5 4 3 2 1

Book design by Kathie S. Rickard
Cover design by Susan Olinsky
Book production by Wiley Publishing, Inc. Composition Services
Wiley Bicentennial Logo: Richard J. Pacifico

We seldom seem to get the perfect gift: The color is wrong, the size is too small, or it's just not our style. Ten years ago, my husband, Terry, brought home the perfect gift: a Jack Russell Terrier puppy we named Molly. You never know where life will take you, and that one small gift changed the course of my life. I want to dedicate this book to Terry. Thank you for your love, your encouragement, and, most of all, your support in all I have done—for knowing what I need before I want it, and for finding the tenacious terrier who changed our lives.

About the Author

Jean M. Fogle is a freelance writer and photographer who specializes in dogs and gardens. Her photographs have appeared in Browntrout, Willow Creek Press, Reiman Publications, and Petprints calendars, and her articles have been published in *Woman's Day, Dog Fancy, Popular Dogs,* and other national magazines. She is a member of the Dog Writers Association of America and can be found at www.jeanmfogle.com. She lives in the Shenandoah Valley of Virginia with her husband, Terry, and their Jack Russell Terrier, Molly.

Preface

When Molly, my Jack Russell Terrier, was six months old, I took her to the beach for the first time. From her initial step in the sand until the moment I dragged her away to head for home, it was apparent that the beach was heaven on earth to my terrier. Seeing her spontaneity and joy liberated me. As she dashed headlong into the waves, I felt the stress of the day melt away and felt laughter tumble from my throat. Together we met many friends—and no strangers.

Glancing out to sea, I noticed a surfer getting ready to put his Golden Retriever on his surfboard. Thrusting Molly into the arms of a new friend, I grabbed my camera and ran. Wading out as deep into the water as I dared, I started taking pictures. As I clicked away, the surfer positioned his dog on the board and pushed him into a wave. With a huge canine grin, the Golden rode the wave until it folded over him and only a nose peeked through the surf. Wading back to shore, I knew that I had gotten some good shots.

From those photos forward, I was hooked. For the past eight years, I have haunted the beach with Molly by my side, capturing the incredible zest for life that dogs seem to exude there.

When you think about it, we ask a lot of our dogs. Continually conforming to the human world has to be tiring. Being at the beach gives dogs the opportunity to be, well, dogs. At the beach, they can take a break from the rules of home and act in instinctual ways. It has all the ingredients of a perfect environment: toys to retrieve, waves to tackle, smells to explore, friends to romp with, and, most of all, quality time with their favorite humans. Tails gyrating with glee, they dig in the sand, stick their paws into the water, or explode into the waves. Just seeing dogs living in the moment is enough to put a smile on any pet parent's face. At the beach, dogs demonstrate their love of life and remind us to enjoy each day.

No matter what breed of dog you share a home with, you are sure to smile when you see the canine capers depicted on these pages. From the brave to the timid, the big to the small, the swimmer to the digger, all these salty dogs enjoy the beach!

Jean M Fogle

In order to really *enjoy* a dog, one doesn't merely try to train him to be semihuman. The point of it is to open oneself to the possibility of *becoming* partly a dog.

—Edward Hoagland

Most of us, I suppose, are a little *nervous* of the sea.

No matter what its smiles may be, we
doubt its friendship.

—H. M. Tomlinson

Praise the sea; on *shore* remain.

—John Florio

Every time you *smile* at someone, it is an action of love,

a *gift* to that person,

a beautiful thing.

—Mother Teresa

Heaven is under our feet as well as over our heads.

—Henry David Thoreau

You will do *foolish* things, but do them with **enthusiasm**.

—Colette

Speak softly and carry a big *stick*.

—Theodore Roosevelt

We don't *stop playing* because we grow old,

we *grow old* because we stop playing.

—George Bernard Shaw

I think we are drawn to dogs because they are the *uninhibited* creatures

we might be if we weren't certain we
knew better.

—George Bird Evans

The best way out is always *through*.

—Robert Frost

There is no end. There is no beginning.
There is only the *infinite passion* of life.

—Federico Fellini

I believe that one of life's greatest risks
is never *daring* to risk.

—Oprah Winfrey

Diligence is the mother of good fortune.

—Miguel de Cervantes

Slow down and enjoy life. It's not only the scenery you miss by going too fast—you also miss the sense of where you are going and *why*.

—Eddie Cantor

Ride on! Rough-shod if need be,

smooth-shod if that will do, but ride on!

—Charles Dickens

We act as though *comfort* and luxury were
the chief requirements of life,

when all that we need to make us really happy is something to be *enthusiastic* about.

—Charles Kingsley

Whoever said you can't buy happiness
forgot about little *puppies*.

—Gene Hill

It's not the *size* of the dog in the fight,

it's the size of the *fight* in the dog.

—Mark Twain

If you can attain **repose** and *calm*,

believe that you have seized happiness.

—Julie-Jeanne-Eleanore de Lespinasse

Anyone can hold the helm when the sea is *calm*.

—Publilius Syrus

Shake off your blunders.

—Og Mandino

Courage is *holding on* a minute longer.

—George S. Patton

The **cautious** seldom err.

—Confucius

Happiness depends upon *ourselves*.

—Aristotle

Very *little* is needed to make a happy life.

—Marcus Aurelius Antoninus

Strangers are friends you have yet to meet.

—Anonymous

Quarrel? Nonsense; we have not quarreled.

If one is not to get into a rage sometimes,

what is the good of being *friends?*

—George Eliot

Nothing sharpens sight like *envy*.

—Thomas Fuller

Nothing's *better* than the wind to your back,

the sun in front of you,

and your *friends* beside you.

—Aaron Douglas Trimble

Dig where the *gold* is . . .

unless you just need some *exercise*.

—John M. Capozzi

In every real man a *child*

is hidden that wants to *play*.

—Friedrich Nietzsche

On with the dance! Let *joy* be unconfined.

—Lord Byron

It is not living, but *living well*,

which we ought to consider most important.

—Plato

All animals except man know that the
ultimate in life is to **enjoy** it.

—Samuel Butler

The sea hates a *coward!*

—Eugene O'Neill

For man, as for flower and beast and bird,
the supreme *triumph* is to be most vividly,

most perfectly *alive*.

—D. H. Lawrence

The best and most *beautiful* things in
the world cannot be seen or even touched—they
must be *felt* with the heart.

—Helen Keller

My strength lies solely in my *tenacity*.

—Louis Pasteur

Energy and *persistence*

conquer all things.

—Benjamin Franklin

My best friend is the one who brings out the *best* in me.

—Henry Ford

The great pleasure of a dog is that you may

make a *fool* of yourself with him and

not only will he not scold you,

but he will make a fool of *himself* too.

—Samuel Butler

The dog was created especially for children.

He is the god of *frolic*.

—Henry Ward Beecher

Tell me who your *friends* are and

I'll tell you who *you* are.

—Assyrian proverb

Enthusiasm finds the opportunities, and

energy makes the most of them.

—Henry Hoskins

It isn't by *size* that you win or fail—

be the *best* of whatever you are.

—Douglas Malloch

Happiness is not a destination,

it is a *method of life*.

—Burton Hills

I am always doing that which I cannot do,

in order that I may *learn* how to do it.

—Pablo Picasso

Everyone who has *run* knows that its most important value is in removing tension and allowing a *release* from whatever other cares the day may bring.

—Jimmy Carter

To a dog, the whole world is a *smell*.

—Anonymous

That they may have a little *peace*, even the

best dogs are compelled to *snarl* occasionally.

—William Feather

Summer afternoon—summer afternoon;
to me those have always been the two most beautiful words
in the English language.

—Henry James

A friend may well be reckoned the

masterpiece of Nature.

—Ralph Waldo Emerson